Pat's Pool Designs, LLC

v.

Desi Dazzle and

Delgado Pool Architects, LLC

Case File
Trial Materials

PAT'S POOL DESIGNS, LLC

V.

DESI DAZZLE AND DELGADO POOL ARCHITECTS, LLC

Case File
Trial Materials

Hon. Christopher T. Whitten
Superior Court of Arizona in Maricopa County

Corynn Gates

NITA®
NATIONAL INSTITUTE FOR TRIAL ADVOCACY

Address inquiries to:
Reprint Permission
National Institute for Trial Advocacy
325 W. South Boulder Rd., Ste. 1
Louisville, CO 80027-1130
Phone: (800) 225-6482
Email: publications@nita.org

ISBN 979-8-88669-172-6
FBA 2172
eISBN 979-8-88669-173-3
eFBA 2173

ASPEN
PUBLISHING

Official co-publisher of NITA.
aspenpublishing.com/NITA

Contents

INTRODUCTION

The case of *Pat's Pool Designs, LLC v. Desi Dazzle & Delgado Pool Architects, LLC* centers on allegations of contractual breach and business interference. Pat's Pool Designs specializes in installing custom pool systems. The company hired Desi Dazzle as a salesperson, later promoting Dazzle to vice president of sales. As part of the employment process, Dazzle signed an agreement containing nonsolicitation, noncompetition, and nondisclosure provisions. The central conflict arose when Dazzle resigned from Pat's Pool Designs and took a similar executive position with Delgado Pool Architects, a direct competitor. Plaintiff alleges that Dazzle took confidential materials such as customer lists and used them to benefit Delgado Pool Architects.

Shortly after Dazzle's departure, Delgado Pool Architects secured a major contract with Mega Builders, Inc., a deal that Plaintiff had been actively negotiating. Plaintiff claims that the loss of the Mega Builders project, which involved 210 pool installations valued at $13.15 million, was directly caused by the wrongful interference of the Defendants. Plaintiff also alleges that Dazzle solicited former colleagues to leave their positions and encouraged existing clients to terminate or redirect contracts. Plaintiff seeks damages for the financial impact of the lost contract, future business losses, and attorneys' fees.

Defendants deny improper solicitation, asserting that employees and clients who transitioned to Delgado Pool Architects did so of their own volition. Furthermore, Defendants contend that Pat's Pools' agreement with Mega Builders was too speculative to support a claim for wrongful interference.

[Optionally, Plaintiff has applied for a preliminary injunction. It claims that Defendants' tortious conduct is clear and that Plaintiff will suffer irreparable injury unless the Court enjoins Defendants from continuing their illegal activity.]

The parties stipulate the following:

- All documents are authentic and meet the requirements of the Original Documents Rule. Other requirements for later admissibility must be established by offering counsel.
- Depositions have been signed under oath.
- Pleadings were signed and timely filed.
- The Pat's Pools employee handbook was attached to Exhibit 4 when it was sent. The handbook is omitted from this case file for the sake of brevity; the pertinent clauses appear at Exhibit 1. No other employee handbook clauses are in dispute.

This case will be tried on liability only unless you are otherwise directed. If the case file will be tried on liability and damages, expect to direct and cross-examine expert witnesses using the expert reports at the end of this case file.

This case file is completely fictitious and any resemblance to any person living or dead is coincidental.

All years in these materials are stated in the following form:

1) YR-0 indicates the actual year in which the case is being tried (i.e., the present year);

2) YR-1 indicates the next preceding year (please use the actual year);

3) YR-2 indicates the second preceding year (please use the actual year), etc.

Electronic exhibits can be found at the following website:

bit.ly/43axcZr
Password: Pats1

Plaintiff's Attorney
654 Central Avenue
Nita City, Nita 85013

SUPERIOR COURT OF NITA
DARROW COUNTY

PAT'S POOL DESIGNS, LLC Plaintiff, v. DESI DAZZLE & DELGADO POOL ARCHITECTS, LLC Defendants	Case No.: CV01-67318 COMPLAINT

Plaintiff, Pat's Pool Designs, LLC, by and through undersigned counsel, and for its COMPLAINT alleges as follows:

JURISDICTION, VENUE, AND PARTIES

1. Pat's Pool Designs, LLC ("Pat's") is a limited liability company, formed under the laws of Nita with a principal place of business in Nita City.

2. Lynn Lasery is the owner and president of Pat's.

3. Delgado Pool Architects LLC ("Delgado") is a limited liability company, formed under the laws of Nita with a principal place of business in Nita City and regularly conducts business in Nita City.

4. Domi Gianni is the owner and president of Delgado.

5. Desi Dazzle is a private person who resided at all relevant times in Nita City.

6. All actions and omissions alleged herein occurred in Nita City.

7. Jurisdiction and venue are proper in this court as all parties reside or conduct business in Nita City and all acts or omissions occurred in Nita City.

GENERAL ALLEGATIONS

8. Pat's is in the business of designing and installing specialized swimming pool systems.

9. Pat's maintains a customer list that includes home designers, builders, and remodelers. This customer list includes information that is not readily available to the public, including, but not limited to, clients' and potential clients' private phone numbers, children's names, lunch orders, etc.

10. On September 11, YR-10, Pat's hired Desi Dazzle to be a salesperson.

11. As part of the onboarding of all new employees, including Desi Dazzle, Pat's provides an employment handbook to the new employee. This handbook includes a nonsolicitation provision, a noncompetition provision, and a nondisclosure provision. All new employees are required to acknowledge each of these provisions separately by initialing each provision. As a condition of their employment, each new employee is also required to sign a form indicating that they agree to be bound by all of the provisions (the "agreement"). Desi Dazzle initialed each of these provisions and signed the agreement to be bound by all of the provisions.

12. The nonsolicitation provision provides:

    Employee agrees that employee shall not, while employed by Pat's and for a period of twelve (12) months following any termination of employment by Pat's, either directly or indirectly:

    a. solicit or assist any other person or entity in the solicitation of Pat's employees, known customers, or known potential customers to leave their employment or cancel their contracts with Pat's, or

    b. solicit or assist any other person or entity in the solicitation of Pat's vendors or suppliers to cancel their contracts with Pat's.

13. The noncompetition provision provides:

    Employee agrees that employee shall not, while employed by Pat's and for a period of six (6) months following any termination of employment by Pat's, either directly or indirectly, solicit or provide pool design or installation services to any person or entity that:

    a. was a customer of Pat's at the time the employment with Pat's terminated, and

    b. does business within a five (5) mile radius of the Nita City town limits.

14. The nondisclosure provision provides:

    Employee agrees and acknowledges that employment with Pat's allows access to trade secrets, including confidential information and special knowledge of Pat's customer lists, business methods, and organization, disclosure of which would be harmful to Pat's if made known to any business competitor. Employee agrees that, both during the term of employment and after termination of employment, employee will not disclose to any other person or entity Pat's trade secrets or confidential information, including but not limited to its customer lists, business methods, and organization.

15. Desi Dazzle continued as an employee of Pat's, being promoted from salesperson to vice president of sales in YR-5.

16. Desi Dazzle was involved in negotiations between Pat's and Mega Builder, Inc. for Pat's to design and install pool systems in a subdivision of homes being constructed by Mega Builders, Inc.

17. These negotiations had progressed to such a stage that Pat's and Mega Builders, Inc. both signed a letter of intent on October 31, YR-2, for Pat's to design and install 210 private pools and 3 community pools.

18. The letter of intent called for Mega Builders, Inc. to pay Pat's $13.15 million.

19. The letter of intent was signed by the Annie Dietz, vice president of purchasing for Mega Builders, Inc. and by Desi Dazzle on behalf of Pat's.

20. In early December YR-2, management at Pat's learned that Desi Dazzle was taking steps to go to work for Delgado, one of Pat's largest competitors. Pat's immediately took reasonable steps to enforce its restrictive covenants.

21. On December 7, YR-2, Desi Dazzle resigned from employment with Pat's.

22. Upon information and belief, Desi Dazzle took a copy of the protected customer list, which was the property of Pat's, when leaving Pat's employment.

23. Upon information and belief, Desi Dazzle took a job as the vice president of sales with Delgado on or before January 3, YR-1.

24. Upon learning that Desi Dazzle had taken a job with Delgado, Lynn Lasery sent an email to Domi Gianni advising that there were contractual prohibitions that prevented Desi Dazzle from competing, soliciting, or disclosing information. A copy of the employee handbook was included in that email.

25. Upon information and belief, in December YR-2, and the three months that followed, Desi Dazzle solicited other employees of Pat's to leave employment with Pat's and go to work for Delgado.

26. Upon information and belief, in December YR-2, and the three months that followed, Desi Dazzle contacted and solicited people and entities that were customers of Pat's to stop doing business with Pat's and instead do business with Delgado.

27. Upon information and belief, Desi Dazzle has shared with Delgado details about Pat's customer lists and its business methods and organization, all in violation of the agreement.

28. Mega Builders, Inc. informed Pat's on January 21, YR-1, that it no longer intended to enter into a contract with Pat's for the design and installation of pool systems.

29. Upon information and belief, Delgado entered into a contract with Mega Builders, Inc. sometime in December YR-2, that was the same as described in the October 31, YR-2, letter of intent—to design and install 210 private pools and 3 community pools.

COUNT 1—BREACH OF CONTRACT
(AGAINST DESI DAZZLE)

30. The agreement is a valid, written, and enforceable contract between Desi Dazzle and Pat's.

31. The nonsolicitation, nondisclosure, and noncompetition clauses are material terms of that contract.

32. By sharing Pat's customer list with Delgado, soliciting Pat's employees and customers, and directly competing with Pat's, Desi Dazzle breached the contract.

33. As a direct and proximate result of Desi Dazzle's breach, Pat's has suffered, and continues to suffer, damages.

COUNT 2—TORTIOUS INTERFERENCE
WITH CONTRACT AND BUSINESS EXPECTANCIES
(AGAINST DESI DAZZLE AND DELGADO)

34. Upon information and belief, both Desi Dazzle and Delgado knew before January 1, YR-1, that Pat's had entered into a letter of intent with Mega Builders, Inc. to design and install 210 private pools and 3 community pools.

35. Upon information and belief, Desi Dazzle and Delgado interfered with Pat's reasonable expectations that it would enter into a contract with Mega Builders, Inc. by soliciting Mega Builders, Inc. to contract with Delgado for substantially the same work.

36. As a direct and proximate result of that interference, Pat's has suffered, and continues to suffer, damages.

PRAYERS FOR RELIEF

WHEREFORE, Plaintiff prays that this court enter judgment in its favor and against the Defendants, as follows:

1. For actual past damages sustained by Plaintiff that are shown to have resulted from the unlawful actions of the Defendants;

2. For future damages by Plaintiff that are shown to have resulted from the unlawful acts of the Defendants;
3. For all costs and attorney fees incurred by Plaintiff to prosecute this action; and
4. For pre-judgment interest and post-judgment interest on the foregoing sums.
5. For injunctive relief, as the court sees fit.

Dated this [DATE]

____

(ATTORNEY NAME)

Defendants' Attorney
123 Main Street
Nita City, Nita 85032

SUPERIOR COURT OF NITA
DARROW COUNTY

PAT'S POOL DESIGNS, LLC Plaintiff, v. DESI DAZZLE, et al. Defendants	Case No.: CV01-67318 ANSWER

Defendants Desi Dazzle and Delgado Pool Architects, LLC ("Delgado"), by and through undersigned counsel and for its ANSWER, admit, deny, and allege as follows:

JURISDICTION, VENUE, AND PARTIES

1. The Defendants are without sufficient information to form a belief as to the allegations contained in paragraphs 1 and 2 of Plaintiff's Complaint and therefore deny the same.

2. Defendants admit the allegations contained in paragraphs 3, 4, 5, 6, and 7 of Plaintiff's Complaint.

GENERAL ALLEGATIONS

3. The Defendants are without sufficient information to form a belief as to the allegations contained in paragraph 8 of Plaintiff's Complaint, but do not contest the same.

4. The Defendants are without sufficient information to form a belief as to the allegations contained in paragraphs 9, 10, 11, 12, 13, and 14 of Plaintiff's Complaint and therefore deny the same. They admit that Plaintiff correctly quoted the language cited but deny that the restrictive covenants are legally enforceable.

5. The Defendants are without sufficient information to form a belief as to the allegations contained in paragraphs 15 and 16 of Plaintiff's Complaint and therefore deny the same.

6. The Defendants admit the allegations contained in paragraphs 17, 18, and 19 of Plaintiff's Complaint, but note that Desi Dazzle's involvement in the negotiations was minimal.

7. The Defendants are without sufficient information to form a belief as to the allegations contained in paragraphs 20, 21, and 22 of Plaintiff's Complaint and therefore deny the same.

8. The Defendants admit the allegations contained in paragraph 23 of Plaintiff's Complaint.

9. The Defendants are without sufficient information to form a belief as to the allegations contained in paragraph 24 of Plaintiff's Complaint and therefore deny the same.

10. The Defendants deny the allegations contained in paragraphs 25, 26, and 27 of Plaintiff's Complaint.

11. The Defendants are without sufficient information to form a belief as to the allegations contained in paragraph 28 of Plaintiff's Complaint and therefore deny the same.

12. The Defendants admit the allegations contained in paragraph 29 of Plaintiff's Complaint.

BREACH OF CONTRACT

13. The Defendants deny the allegations contained in paragraphs 30, 31, 32, and 33 of Plaintiff's Complaint.

14. The Defendants affirmatively allege that the restrictive covenants Plaintiff seeks to enforce do not comply with the law and are therefore not enforceable.

INTERFERENCE WITH BUSINESS EXPECTANCY

15. The Defendants admit the allegations contained in paragraph 34 of Plaintiff's Complaint.

16. The Defendants deny the allegations contained in paragraphs 35 and 36 of Plaintiff's Complaint.

17. The Defendants affirmatively allege that there was no enforceable contract between Plaintiff and Mega Builders, Inc. and any expectation that there would be such a contract was not reasonable.

WHEREFORE, the Defendants pray for the following relief:

1. That Plaintiff's Complaint be dismissed with prejudice;

2. That Plaintiff be ordered to pay all of Defendants' attorney fees and costs; and

3. That Defendants be awarded any further relief that the court deems just and reasonable.

Dated this [DATE]

____

(ATTORNEY NAME)

Deposition of Desi Dazzle

My name is Desi Dazzle. I live in Nita City, Nita. I have a BA in art history with a concentration in computer science from Nita State University and a master's degree in business engineering, also from Nita State. I have worked in the pool design and construction industry for more than a decade, including positions in design, engineering, marketing, and sales.

I began my career at Pretty Pools, where I learned construction logistics, graphic design, and sales. In YR-10, I accepted a sales position at Pat's Pool Designs, LLC ("Pat's"). I was promoted to vice president of sales in YR-5. When I started working, Pat's HR department gave me onboarding documents that I now know included a nonsolicitation clause, a noncompete provision, and a nondisclosure agreement. Those are my initials and signature on Exhibit 1, the documents provided by Pat's, but I did not read those provisions in detail when I signed them because I had already begun working there and thought they were just formalities.

When I started, Pat's business model focused on single-family projects. I felt that Pat's needed to think bigger. I urged Lynn Lasery, the owner of Pat's, to focus on larger projects, including multi-family developments. I suggested a plan to appeal to the multi-family developer by offering to install base model pools that builders could include in the initial home price. We could then upsell individual homeowners on higher-end options and add-ons. Just like upgrading cabinets and flooring, buyers could upgrade their pools and roll the price into their mortgage. Pat's would not get paid a lot for the design and construction of the base model pool but could make a lot of money if homeowners agreed to upgrades. In addition, Pat's would not face any of the financing risk because we would get our money upfront. Of course, everyone loved my idea. We got a great brochure designed that showcased our upgrades, and the idea took off. After my idea worked on that first multi-family development, I was promoted to vice president of sales in YR-5.

In YR-2, Pat's Pools had a chance to win a really big project with Mega Builders, Inc. Mega Builders was planning a huge residential development, and they anticipated 210 of the houses having private pools as well as 3 community pools in the development. I was not super involved with this project. Lynn wanted a new employee with a pretty good-looking résumé to run the business plan for the Mega Builders project. The guy's name was Allen Snyder, Pat's hotshot new CFO. I was a little taken aback to be put under this person, but I'm a team player. I went to Snyder with a great sales pitch, mockups of brochures, and a whole sales plan that he could just approve and take all the credit. Snyder rejected proposal after proposal, including tiered pricing, upgrade incentives to homeowners, and profit sharing on upgrades with the builders. Allen wanted to use an old-school pricing model that most other pool companies used because it was "tried and true." Completely ignoring all the success Pat's had seen with my sales plans. Allen lacked vision. The whole process frustrated me.

Under the contract Snyder offered to Mega Builders, Pat's would build 210 boring, basic model pools for homes in the subdivision. That is a lot of pools—think of the opportunities to upsell! No one builds 200-plus houses all at once before anyone moves in, so you build a great pool for the model home, landscape it like a dream, and you're already halfway to upselling beautiful pools. They practically sell themselves. As homes get built and people see the different pools, even more are going to want something better than a square hole in the ground with a concrete surround. The real estate agents love it because they're selling the dream and a great pool is part of it. But no. Snyder was all about the safe money, the sure thing. No vision. I think he scared Lynn into playing it safe.

No, I don't know exactly how much profit Pat's made on the projects I won with my upsell method. I mean, yeah, it required more design time for Pat's because buyers wanted this tweaked or that changed. We had to stay involved with a development project for much longer because we couldn't just assembly-line build a hundred pools and walk away. And yeah, it's probably more expensive my way. I don't know. I'm not the numbers guy. But I do know that it got us lots of referrals—people calling to say that they saw one of our pools at a friend's house and could we build one for them. That's additional profit you gotta figure in. Lynn was excited because there was so much imagination involved. You get into pool design because you love it. Heck, even our installers loved the upsell because their work was so interesting and they got to make beautiful pools. And then Snyder came along and wrecked it.

Based on Snyder's initial pitch, Mega Builders signed a nonbinding letter of intent on October 31, YR-2. Snyder was out the day the letter of intent was prepared, so I signed it on behalf of Pat's. I didn't like signing it, but Lynn had rejected my ideas, so I signed. The letter of intent was for an agreed-upon amount of $13.15 million. Exhibit 2 is a true and accurate copy of that letter of intent that I signed.

At the end of October YR-2, Pat's sent me to vend at a builders conference. Delgado Pool Architects had a booth there as well, and I talked to the owner, Domi Gianni. This wasn't unusual. You talk business and compare notes with all the vendors in between talking to the conference attendees. Everyone knows everyone at these events and Domi is an old friend. We talked shop for a while and eventually got around to discussing my feelings about Snyder and the general direction of Pat's. Domi asked whether I would be interested in joining the Delgado team. I said I hadn't ever considered it, but I'd think about it. I wasn't really thinking that hard about it, but I'd had to go back to Pat's to sign that letter of intent and when I got back to the building conference I was a little steamed about the whole thing. So it was that day, October 31, YR-2, that Domi and I began exchanging emails. Exhibit 3 shows copies of some of the emails I exchanged with Domi right after the conference and in the weeks that followed.

The more I thought about the wasted opportunity with Mega Builders, the more frustrated I got. I tried to be a team player. I took my list of upgrades to Snyder, suggesting that Pat's at least contact the home buyers with options for upgrades, but Snyder brushed me off—that wasn't our business; we just dig holes and dump concrete in them. No, that's not exactly what he said. It was more like, "Stay out of this, we just build pools," but it was the same thing to me.

There was no contract between Pat's and Mega Builders, and I knew Mega Builders would love my ideas that Snyder rejected. I figured the project was fair game. On November 1, YR-2, I sent

Domi an email and asked to go to dinner to talk about the Delgado Pool Architects vision. At dinner, Domi offered me a job with a 25 percent pay increase. I said that I needed to think about it. Domi asked if I had signed any agreement that prevented me from moving to a different sales team. I told Domi that I might have, but I couldn't be certain because I didn't read the fine print in some documents that they asked me to sign a while after I started at Pat's.

Prior to my start date, I told Domi several of my ideas for pricing and product enhancements—the same ideas Snyder had rejected in the Mega Builders negotiations. I did not take any physical or electronic files from Pat's, nor did I copy or retain the company's customer list. I do, however, know many of the names, phone numbers, and personal information of Pat's customers. I also know that kind of information about many of my former coworkers. I stored that information in my phone and in my personal calendar because I consider them friends.

I also have lots of extra information about many of those people stored in my phone and calendar—things like birthdays, kids' names, and coffee orders. This extra information allowed me to make those people feel special when I talked to them. I cultivated those relationships and collected that information myself. That wasn't anything Pat's gave me or would ever have without me. Yeah, there was a database when I came on, but it was barebones. Maybe half a dozen spouses' names, a few kids. Nothing about who loves golf, who plays tennis, who has a boat or a ski condo. Spouse and kid names are expected; people really love it when you remember those more personal things about them. Pat's database was clunky, with a nightmare interface, so I kept all this info on my phone. No, not a company phone—Lynn didn't provide those. This was on my personal phone. Of course, I continued to talk to many of these people after leaving Pat's. You get to know them as friends after a while. You get to know their spouses, you go out to dinner as couples, not just two business associates.

After additional discussions, I decided to resign from Pat's on December 7, YR-2, and accepted a position at Delgado, where I began work as vice president of sales on January 3, YR-1.

On December 14, YR-2, I put up a post on my socials congratulating Delgado Pool Architects after learning Domi had a great first call with the folks at Mega Builders. I posted that I couldn't wait to work with a real innovator and the best design team in the business. I posted on Linque, Z, Snap-Talk, and FriendMe. The post on Z went sort of viral—it had 12,666 likes. That is Exhibit 5. After that, my phone started ringing continually. I received calls from customers and employees from Pat's who were interested in working with Domi. I told them I wasn't employed with Delgado yet and that they had to wait. Some people asked me to let them know when I officially started, so I made those calls once I got settled in.

After joining Delgado, I worked to develop new business opportunities, including a successful contract with Mega Builders. I had no formal role in those negotiations. Domi led the negotiations but welcomed my input. I guess you could say I was the main advisor. I shared many of the ideas that Snyder had rejected. Mega Builders loved my ideas. They sealed the deal.

That vision is why, after I started with Delgado, two friends and former colleagues from Pat's—MJ Barr and Monique Carter—reached out to me about working at Delgado. They said they saw Delgado's recruiting ad and asked if working here was really that good. I said absolutely, and gave Domi their contact information, but I did not push them to quit Pat's at all. I did tell them how generous Domi was in setting compensation, what a great working environment there was at Delgado, all the innovation I was getting to do, and how much I'd enjoy working with them again. But I didn't need to convince or pressure them at all.

Several smaller clients that used Pat's for pool maintenance and servicing, including Haden Hotels and Rocker Resorts, later became Delgado customers. I did not contact them prior to starting work for Delgado. After that, however, I sent the CFOs of lots of companies multiple emails and texts to let them know how much I loved my new position at Delgado. Again, those were contacts that I had personally saved over the years, not from any customer list. Haden Hotels and Rocker Resorts got in touch with me and I told them what a great company Delgado was and how reliable the company is.

I make this statement voluntarily and under oath to clarify my actions and intent during the relevant.

Signed under oath,
Desi Dazzle
January 2, YR-0

DEPOSITION OF ALLEN SNYDER III

My name is Allen Snyder III. My résumé is attached as Exhibit 8. I graduated from Stanford University with a bachelor's degree in business finance at age 18 and a master's degree in finance with a concentration in construction project management at age 20. Yes, you heard that right.

After working in both finance and design capacities for several construction firms, I joined Pat's Pool Designs, LLC as chief financial officer in YR-3. I accepted this position at Pat's in part to remain in Nita City to assist with family medical obligations.

My responsibilities at Pat's included budget forecasting, cost modeling, and strategic pricing. In late YR-2, Lynn Lasery, the company's president, asked me to take the lead on preparing a proposal for a contract with Mega Builders, Inc. to design and install 210 private pools and 3 community pools in a new development. Lynn said that although Desi Dazzle had previously led similar projects, I would lead this one. Good decision, in my humble opinion.

When Lynn and I met about the Mega Builders project, Lynn explained that Pat's had traditionally used a "fool-proof" method of setting bid pricing on new projects. It estimated how much it would cost to construct the project and added 10 percent. That was the bid amount. I liked the idea, but I thought we could increase the desirability and ultimately the profitability by adding a few novel concepts to the bid proposal. I suggested to Lynn that we include discounts for Mega Builders if they paid early in the construction. I also suggested offering Mega Builders upgraded landscaping for each of the community pools. Lynn told me that landing the project would likely result in a bonus for me—one which never materialized, thanks to Desi.

Desi fought me on this approach and wanted a more speculative model; one that relied on consumer upgrades and variable enhancements. I reviewed Desi's proposals and thought they were incompatible with the risk tolerance and financial expectations of Mega Builders. Of course, Lynn supported my recommendation to proceed with a more conservative structure. Frankly, under Desi's proposal, Pat's could go bankrupt if homeowners didn't purchase upgrades to their pools. I'm not exaggerating when I say Desi was gambling with Lynn's money, and I told Lynn just that. Yes, it had worked out well with some projects Desi led, but others came in lower than a straight, traditional contract. Pat's never lost money on any of the deals, but I could pinpoint individual houses where buyers didn't upgrade and Pat's built those pools at a loss. Also, the housing bubble can't last forever. A bid like Desi's could ruin the company. It was a lot of additional work for the payoff Pat's received, in my opinion. Why expose yourself to that much risk?

I facilitated the meetings with Mega Builders and they seemed pleased with the terms I proposed. In our meeting on October 31, YR-2, Mega Builders agreed to sign a letter of intent. The meeting ran long and I needed to get home to help my parents. I had to leave before the letter of intent was finalized, so I asked Desi to sign the final letter. I figured Desi was capable of handling at least that task. Exhibit 2 is a copy of the letter of intent I drafted, which has Desi's signature.

After the parties signed, Desi called me and again tried to argue that we should incorporate upgrade sales directly to the homeowners. I was exhausted. I snapped and said something like "Dammit, Desi, this project is mine, not yours! We are pricing it my way. Please leave this project to me." At least I said please.

In early November, Lynn and I went to dinner at the Old Biscuit Factory with Annie Dietz, the owner of Mega Builders and her VP—I don't recall their name. The deal was secure and Mega Builders was very satisfied with the terms of the contract. Mega Builders loved the incentives I built into the proposal. At the end of dinner, Dietz said, "We look forward to signing on the dotted line." When we left the restaurant, Lynn was elated and said, "There is a big year-end bonus coming your way." That seemed fair, given all I had done.

Over the holiday season, Mega Builders continued to express interest and confirmed their intention to finalize a contract. Exhibit 6 is one of those messages, which I'd forwarded to Lynn.

In early January YR-1, out of nowhere, Annie Dietz sent me a message indicating they would be contracting with a different pool company. That text is part of Exhibit 7.

I stormed through the office to show Lynn the text. I was so mad that I had steam coming out of my ears. I just handed my phone to Lynn, who immediately called Annie Dietz. She didn't answer so Lynn texted using my phone: "What the heck Annie?! We had an agreement. Who are you using?" It's hard to describe Lynn's reaction when the response appeared: "We didn't have a contract. We are going with Delgado." Those are also in Exhibit 7.

I had no knowledge at the time that Desi had accepted a position with Delgado. I was not involved in any post-resignation matters involving Desi's employment there.

I make this statement under oath to explain my involvement in the Mega Builders project and related events.

Signed by Allen Snyder III
Under oath,
January 2, YR-0.

Deposition of Domi Gianni

My name is Domi Gianni. I am the owner and CEO of Delgado Pool Architects, a pool design and installation company. I hold a master's degree in business and finance from Nita State University. Before Delgado, I worked for a venture capital firm, Gates Bills and Coins (GBC). I founded Delgado Pool Architects with investment backing from GBC in YR-11. At the time, the industry was most serviced by sole proprietors or small, closely held companies that refused to change their method of doing business. I saw it as a great business opportunity.

Delgado Pool Architects became successful almost immediately. I swiped a few of the best employees from local pool companies to get the business started. I hired a designer, a general contractor, a salesperson, and I did the rest. The employers of the woman I hired as the pool designer threatened to sue us over a noncompete, but they never did. We immediately made our mark on the industry. We became a well-known, mid-level pool builder by YR-4.

From the beginning, I hired creative and ambitious professionals. Desi came to my attention after we lost several bids to Pat's Pools. I made follow-up calls asking several of these companies why we didn't get their business, and they told me about Desi's creativity. That was more than five years ago. Desi's been on my radar ever since. We've met over the years and I've stayed in contact in hopes that Desi would jump ship at some point.

I finally got my break with Desi in YR-2. We both had booths at a builder's conference and chatted a few times during the first days of the show. Desi came into the vender's room late on October 31, YR-2, and was hopping mad. Usually, Desi talked about how great Pat's was, but this day was very different. Desi was being frozen out by a new guy. Desi was frustrated about a new project Pat's was trying to land with Mega Builders. "I have great ideas about innovative pricing models and no one is listening to me!" Just ranting like that. When the floor closed, I suggested we go get a drink. After a few cocktails, I asked if Desi was interested in leaving. Desi just started crying. I didn't know what to do. I told Desi to go get an Uber and think about it. I said, "I'll get the check. I probably make more money than you do. What are they paying you over there?" Desi said, "I'm okay financially. It's not about the money. It's about being appreciated and valued." I just smiled. It's always about the money.

Later that night, I got an email that was nearly incomprehensible from Desi. The email is Exhibit 4. I knew Desi had been drinking, but wow, spellcheck would have helped. The message of the email was clear, though—Desi was staying with Pat's. But I didn't give up.

Finally, in December, YR-2, I got another email saying Desi had quit and wanted to talk about working for Delgado. After a short negotiation about compensation, Desi accepted an offer to become my VP of sales. Desi wanted to take some time off before starting, so we agreed to a January 7, YR-1, start date.

After resigning from Pat's, but before starting work with Delgado, Desi suggested I pursue a contract with Mega Builders. Desi said that Mega Builders was in discussions with Pat's about a big project, but no contract had been signed. Based on this understanding, Delgado submitted a proposal incorporating our pricing model.

The negotiations with Mega Builders were fast and easy. Mega Builders told me to draw up the contract before the end of the year. We signed the contract on December 30, YR-2. After we sealed the deal with Mega Builders, I knew I needed more talent. I put up a recruiting ad on Linque.

Before even starting, Desi posted on social media praising the new job. What a great post! So great that two of Desi's former colleagues from Pat's, MJ Barr and Monique Carter, reached out independently and were later hired. Like I said, I was advertising, and at least one of them mentioned the recruiting ad. I don't remember what was said, just that they knew we were hiring. We also heard from clients who worked with Desi at Pat's, companies like Haden Hotels and Rocker Resorts, who became our clients.

At some point before Desi's first day, Lynn Lasery emailed me making various threats. That email is Exhibit 4. I reviewed the materials Lynn provided. I honestly thought we were fine and had nothing to worry about. We didn't solicit anyone and Desi didn't do anything wrong as far as I could see.

Competition is the name of the game. After all these years in the business, Lynn should know that. If you want to keep up, hire a new head of sales who has some vision. I mean, c'mon. Your CFO is heading up negotiations? What does a pencil pusher know about selling pools?

I offer this statement voluntarily and under oath.

Signed under oath,
Domi Gianni
January 3, YR-0

Deposition of Lynn Lasery

My name is Lynn Lasery. I am the owner and president of Pat's Pool Designs, LLC. I began working for Pat's in YR-35 and bought the company from the previous owners under a succession plan that began in YR-15 and concluded several years later. I have been the sole owner and leader of the company since YR-12.

After assuming full operational control, one of the first things I did was update our employment policies and agreements to better protect the business. Loyalty isn't what it used to be. So, in YR-11 I met with some employment lawyers and we prepared all new policies and employment agreements. I wanted to safeguard our confidential information, like customer information and preference. I also want to prevent ex-employees from competing with us unfairly or from stealing our employees.

I hired Desi Dazzle as a salesperson in YR-10 based on Desi's reputation for initiative and interest in product development. Desi came on board eager to learn and was thrilled to get our customer database. I had kept that database for years before Desi started. It had more than just names and phone numbers. If I learned the names of a customer's kids or partner, I'd add it in. No, I wasn't methodical about adding—they were things that came up naturally in conversation. After Desi really got going and took the sales calls off my hands, I didn't pay much attention to the database, but the fields were already available.

Desi was a quick learner, and a natural at sales—lots of enthusiasm. A couple years in, Desi came up with a plan to start targeting larger builders as clients. I resisted a bit at first—we were doing a steady business, and it seemed a little risky to stick our necks out—but I have to admit it was a great plan. These contributions earned Desi a promotion to vice president of sales in YR-5. Over time, however, Desi began to resist my direction and do things the Desi way, not mine.

Nita City's building boom was great for business, and in October YR-3, my tax accountant urged me to hire an in-house financial officer. Before that, I'd just kept track of payments and expenses with some free bookkeeping software—no, I wasn't as diligent as I should have been. That's why I was scrambling to get all my documents straight before the October 15 deadline for late filing. The tax accountant explained to me that a CFO would do more than just make sure I filed my taxes on time and paid all my vendors. CFOs look at the overall picture and forecast trends and plan for the future. That sounded smart, considering how much we were growing. The tax accountant recommended Allen Snyder as someone with a good reputation in the industry. I hired Allen right away and he came on at Pat's in late November YR-3.

Allen came on board and thoroughly reviewed all our business records. It was kind of embarrassing when he made it clear that I had done a poor job of running the business, but Allen assured me that he could get everything under control and make Pat's run much more successfully. It's been worth his salary just to free up my time and let me concentrate on the things I got into this business to do.

In spring YR-2, Allen came to me with concerns about our bidding. He made me understand that Desi's way of doing business was much riskier than I had realized. I was pretty sold on Desi's vision, but that's what Desi does, right? A salesperson through and through. Allen showed me the numbers, and while Desi's results were ahead of the traditional bidding process, it wasn't by as much as I had hoped. Allen talked about how if the housing bubble burst we could lose a lot of money building pools under cost in the hopes of upselling to home buyers. I hadn't considered that possibility, but what he said made sense. I didn't immediately change Desi's bidding style, but Allen had me thinking about it.

Toward the end of summer YR-2, we had a great opportunity to bid on a very big project with Mega Builders. They were building a new subdivision that would include hundreds of pools. I wanted to build those pools. It might not sound life-changing, but that project really could have changed my company.

Mega Builders was a conservative company. Its principal, Annie Dietz, did not like risk and appreciated professionalism and certainty. I understood the type of pricing Mega Builders would want and I knew we could secure the contract. I asked Allen to draft a bid. Normally, I would have had Desi do that job, but I thought Allen was a better fit for the Mega Builders bid and we'd win the contract with his approach. I wrote up the draft contract, being the one that knows the business, Allen made some improvements to my ideas, and I ultimately signed off on the terms. No, I didn't discuss the bid or my reason for doing it this way with Desi. I felt a little guilty about that, since Desi was the VP of sales, but Allen pointed out that Pat's is my company and I didn't have to let Desi push me around.

On October 31, YR-2, we executed a letter of intent with Mega Builders. Exhibit 2 is the letter of intent. Due to Allen's scheduling conflict, Desi signed the document on behalf of Pat's.

After the letter of intent was signed, we started ramping up our hiring to make sure that we could deliver on the agreement. Allen was still working with Annie Dietz regarding the finer details of the contract—getting the i's dotted and the t's crossed. Annie Dietz was very clear that Mega Builders agreed to the terms of our contract. Everyone was moving forward on the agreement, because we all knew it was a done deal. I understand we did not have a formal contract, but we had a letter of intent, which is basically a promise to enter the contract. We also received messages from Mega Builders proving the agreement was final. Exhibit 6 includes one of those messages.

Desi quit on December 7, YR-2. While I was sad to part ways, Desi's way of doing business did not fit well with Pat's. It was a little too "outside-the-box" for my taste. When Desi quit, we wished each other well and I specifically pointed out the restrictions Desi had agreed to regarding solicitation, disclosure, and competition. That seems to upset Desi, who simply told me, "Don't worry about it," and left.

Just after Desi quit, I heard through the grapevine that Desi might have already accepted a position with Delgado Pool Architects. When I learned this, I pulled up the employee handbook and emailed it to Domi Gianni, Delgado's owner, pointing out the relevant portions of the handbook. I warned Domi about the nonsolicitation agreements and the noncompete. Exhibit 4 includes emails between me and Domi.

In January YR-1, Mega Builders informed us that they had selected another pool company. Around that same time two of our best architects, MJ Barr and Monique Carter, also quit. When I did my exit interview with them, each said Desi had reached out to them about a better opportunity with Delgado. They called it an opportunity that was too good to let pass. We also lost the pool maintenance and servicing business of two smaller clients, Haden Hotels and Rocker Resorts. I called our contact at each business and was told they wanted to do business with Desi.

These events caused substantial business disruption and financial losses. Pat's is all but done as a company. My entire life has been destroyed. I am angry and lost. I just can't believe this happened. I hope some justice allows Pat's to rebuild from the rubble Desi created.

I make this statement voluntarily and under oath to provide a factual account of the relevant circumstances.

Signed under oath,
Lynn Lasery
January 3, YR-0.

EXHIBITS

Exhibit 1

Excerpts from the Pat's Pools Employment Handbook from Desi Dazzle's Employment File

Section 2.1 of the Restrictive Covenant Agreement provides:

NONSOLICITATION:

Employee agrees that employee shall not, while employed by Pat's and for a period of twelve (12) months following any termination of employment by Pat's, either directly or indirectly:

a. solicit or assist any other person or entity in the solicitation of Pat's employees, known customers, or known potential customers to leave their employment or cancel their contracts with Pat's, or

b. solicit or assist any other person or entity in the solicitation of Pat's vendors or suppliers to cancel their contracts with Pat's.

_______ **Initial**

NONCOMPETE:

Employee agrees that employee shall not, while employed by Pat's and for a period of six (6) months following any termination of employment by Pat's, either directly or indirectly, solicit or provide pool design or installation services to any person or entity that:

a. was a customer of Pat's at the time the employment with Pat's terminated, and

b. does business within a five (5) mile radius of the Nita City town limits.

_______ **Initial**

NONDISCLOSURE:

Employee agrees and acknowledges that employment with Pat's allows access to trade secrets, including confidential information and special knowledge of Pat's customer lists, business methods, and organization, disclosure of which would be harmful to Pat's if made known to any business competitor. Employee agrees that, both during the term of employment and after termination of employment, employee will not disclose to any other person or entity Pat's trade secrets or confidential information, including but not limited to its customer lists, business methods, and organization.

_______ **Initial**

Exhibit 2

Letter of Intent

October 31, YR-2

Mega Builders, Inc.
1234 Foundation Lane
Nita City, Nita 85015

Dear Annie Dietz:

This letter serves as a formal expression of intent to enter into a contract between Pat's Pool Design, LLC and Mega Builders, Inc. for the construction and installation of 210 private pools and 3 community pools at the housing development project of Mega Builders in Nita City.

Consistent with our recent discussion and preliminary planning, Mega Builders agrees to a projected budget of $13.15 million for the pool installations.

Mega Builders is entitled to a 1% discount for paying 25% of the agreed-upon price within 30 days of date of execution of the contract and an additional 2% if 50% of the agreed-upon price is paid within 90 days of the execution of the contract.

Although this letter of intent is nonbinding, the letter reflects the mutual understanding that both parties will proceed in good faith to finalize and execute a formal contract in the coming weeks.

We look forward to working with Mega Builders on this exciting project and are confident that your innovative design and engineering expertise will contribute significantly to its success.

Pat's Pool Design LLC

Desi Dazzle

Mega Builders, Inc.

Annie Dietz

Emails Between Gianni and Dazzle

Desi Dazzle

From:	Domi Gianni <domi@davidspoolarchitects.nita>
Sent:	November 2, YR-2,12:14 AM
To:	Desi Dazzle <dDazzle@patspools.nita>
Subject:	RE: Frustration

Desi,

I hear you. Just . . . think about it. You deserve to be appreciated — and I think we both know your ideas are worth way more than what they're giving you over there.

Let me know if you want to talk more.

– Domi

From:	Desi Dazzle <dDazzle@patspools.nita>
Sent:	October 31, YR-2, 11:58pm
To:	Domi Gianni <domi@davidspoolarchitects.nita>
Subject:	Frustration

Domi,

I'm just really really really anrgey right now. I feel like I'm being pushed aside at Pit's, and its exhausting and demoralizing. I'm putting in soooooooooo much effort, and none of it seems to matter. Allen's taking over everything, and no one is recognizing the work I've done — not the code, not the system, nothing. I appreciate the job offer tonight. Really dude. It made me feel cood to know someone values me, but I love Pat's and love Lynn. So not know . . . maybe someday.

I don't know. Maybe it *is* about the $$$$$$$$$$$$$$$$$$ after all.

– Desii

Desi Dazzle

From:	Desi Dazzle <dDazzle@patspools.nita>
Sent:	November 5, YR-2, 3:45 AM
To:	Domi Gianni <domi@davidspoolarchitects.nita>
Subject:	Let's Talk

Dinner? We should talk. I want to hear more about your vision—and where I might fit into it.

– Desi

Desi Dazzle

From:	Desi Dazzle <dDazzle@patspools.nita>
Sent:	December 7, YR-2, 9:10 AM
To:	Domi Gianni <domi@davidspoolarchitects.nita>
Subject:	Resignation

Domi,

I've officially resigned from Pat's. I'm ready to move forward.

Let's talk next steps.

– Desi

Exhibit 4

Emails Between Lasery and Gianni

Domi Gianni

From: Domi Gianni <domi@davidspoolarchitects.nita>
Date: January 5, YR-1 | 4:47 PM
To: Lynn Lasery <Lynn@patspools.nita>
Subject: Re: Important: Employee Handbook & Nonsolicitation Policy

Hi Lynn,

Thanks for the heads-up and the copy of the handbook. Appreciate the transparency. I took a quick look through the provisions you mentioned—interesting read.

To be clear, I haven't made any formal offers to anyone from Pat's besides Desi. I assumed Desi was in the clear, but I'll definitely take a closer look at what you sent over.

I want to avoid any drama (and legal fees, let's be honest). Desi felt undervalued — I'm just offering a new start.

Let's stay professional on this, yeah?

Best,
Domi Gianni
CEO, Delgado Pool Architects
(819) 555-SWIM

From: Lynn Lasery <Lynn@patspools.nita>
Date: January 5, YR-1 | 9:13 AM
To: Domi Gianni <domi@davidspoolarchitects.nita>
Subject: Important: Employee Handbook & Nonsolicitation Policy
Attachment: PPools_emp_hdbk.docx

Hi Domi,

I'm reaching out because I've heard some rumblings from my team that you hired Desi Dazzle. Unfortunately, Desi is worthless to you because Desi signed a nonsolicitation, noncompete, and nondisclosure agreement. Desi Dazzle cannot contact customers. Desi Dazzle cannot sell pools. And Desi Dazzle cannot take our proprietary information or solicit our customers or employees. I hope you didn't offer to pay Desi too much, because Desi is basically worthless to you.

I'm not going to make assumptions about your plan in hiring Desi, but I want to get ahead of any potential misunderstandings. I've attached a copy of our **employee handbook**. Please note pages 12–14 specifically, which outline our **restrictive covenant agreement**, including **nonsolicitation** and **nondisclosure** provisions.

Thanks for understanding.

Lynn Lasery
President, Pat's Pool Designs
📞 (819) 555-POOL

We design it, build it, and clean it.

Domi Gianni

From:	Lynn Lasery <Lynn@patspools.nita>
Date:	January 6, YR-1 | 8:02 AM
To:	Domi Gianni <domi@davidspoolarchitects.nita>
Subject:	Handbook Follow-Up

Domi,

Appreciate the response but let me be very clear: **if Desi or your team encourages even *one more* employee or client to leave**, we'll have no choice but to pursue this legally.

This isn't personal—it's about protecting the business I've built for 20+ years. I put these clauses in place for a reason.

Consider this email an **official warning**.

–Lynn

Exhibit 5

Desi Dazzle's Z Post

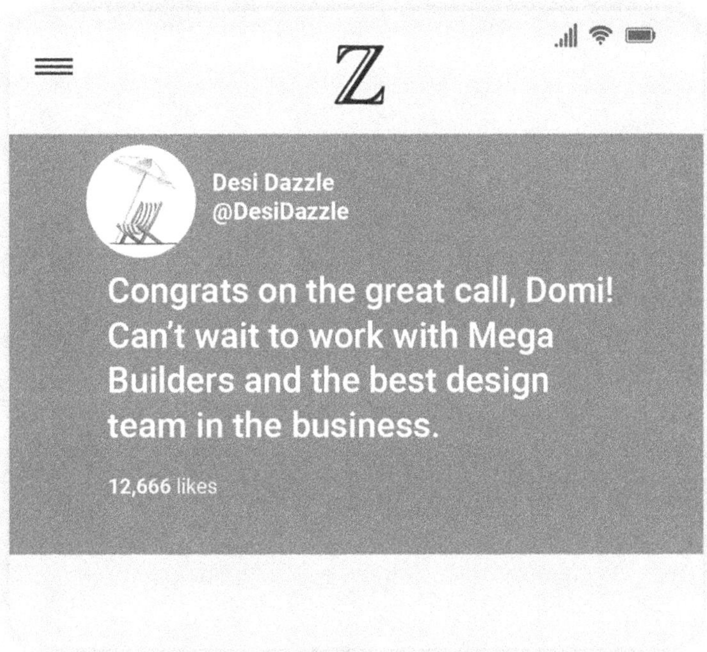

Exhibit 6

Text from Snyder to Lasery Forwarding Message from Dietz

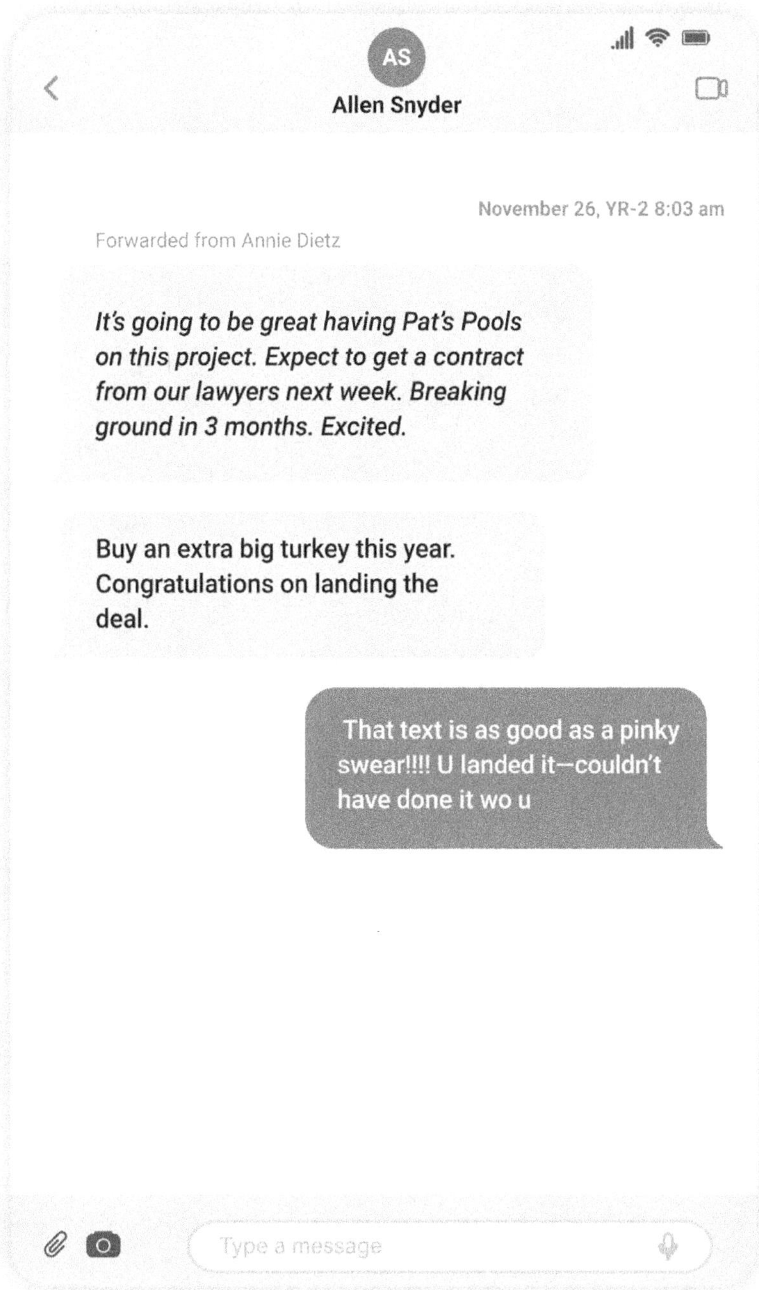

Exhibit 7

Texts Between Dietz and Snyder

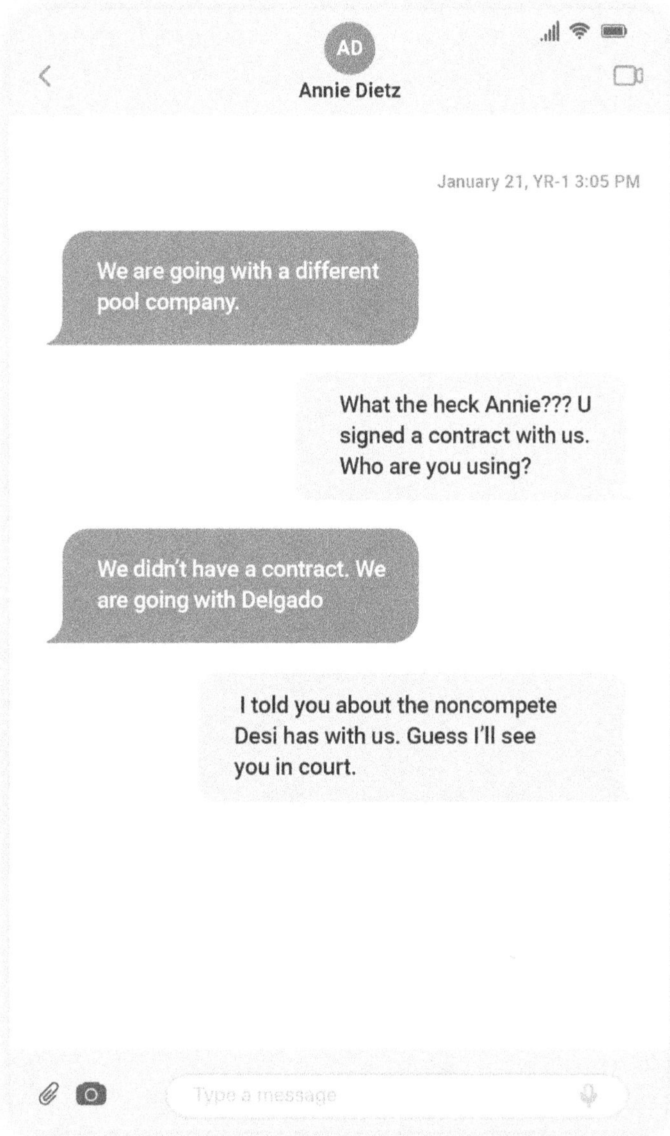

Exhibit 8

Allen Snyder's Résumé

Allen Jefferson Snyder III
Nita City, USA |
(819) 555-4567 |
ajsnyder3@email.nita |
Linque: linque.nita/in/ajsnyder3

Objective: Dedicated and detail-oriented finance and construction professional, seeking a leadership role where I can apply my technical, financial, and design experience to support organizational growth. Passionate about process optimization, cost modeling, and supporting project delivery through sound financial strategy.

Education

- Stanford University—Stanford, CA
    - Master of Science in Finance, Focus: Construction Project Management
    - Completed at age 20
- Stanford University—Stanford, CA
    - Bachelor of Arts in Business Finance
        - Graduated at age 18 | GPA: 3.98
        - Completed 21+ credit hours per semester with additional summer coursework
        - Research assistant on applied finance modeling projects

Work Experience

- Construction Junction—Nita City, USA
  Finance & Design Associate (YR-5 to YR-3)
    - Managed construction cost analysis and budgeting for multi-phase residential builds
    - Supported architectural design teams with layout modeling and feasibility projections
    - Earned 10% salary increase for performance and cross-departmental versatility
- Trager's Construction Company—Nita City, USA
  Finance Assistant-> Design Support Specialist (YR-7 to YR-5)
    - Oversaw budgeting and contractor payment schedules
    - Promoted to support design logistics, collaborating directly with on-site teams
    - Helped reduce cost overruns by 15% through improved project forecasting

Certifications & Achievements

- National Champion, Lincoln Log Construction Competition (Won $10,000 prize at age 8)
- Advanced Excel Modeling for Construction
- AutoCAD & SketchUp Proficiency

Skills

- Construction finance modeling
- Cost +% pricing strategy

SUPERIOR COURT OF NITA
DARROW COUNTY

PAT'S POOL DESIGNS, LLC Plaintiff, v. DESI DAZZLE, et al. Defendants	Case No.: CV01-67318 FINAL JURY INSTRUCTIONS LIABILITY [AND DAMAGES]

You have heard all the testimony and seen all the evidence in this case. It is now time for you to deliberate and make your decision in this matter.

DUTY OF JURORS

It is your duty to determine the facts. You must determine the facts only from the evidence produced in court. Do not guess about any fact. Do not be influenced by sympathy or prejudice. You are the sole judges of the facts. Decide the case by applying the law in these instructions to the facts.

EVIDENCE

You will decide the credibility and weight to be given to any evidence presented in the case, whether it be direct evidence or circumstantial evidence.

CREDIBILITY OF WITNESSES

In deciding the facts of this case, consider what testimony to accept and what to reject. You may accept everything a witness says, or part of it, or none of it.

In evaluating testimony, use the tests for accuracy and truthfulness that people use in determining matters of importance in everyday life, including such factors as: the witness's ability to see or hear or know the things to which the witness testified; the quality of the witness's memory; the witness's manner while testifying; whether the witness has any motive, bias, or prejudice; whether the witness is contradicted by anything the witness said or wrote before trial, or by other evidence; and the reasonableness of the testimony when considered in the light of the other evidence.

Consider all of the evidence in light of reason, common sense, and experience.

EXPERT WITNESSES

A witness qualified as an expert by education or experience may state opinions on matters in that witness's field of expertise and may also state reasons for those opinions.

Judge expert opinion testimony just as any other testimony. You are not bound by it. You may accept or reject it, in whole or in part, and give it as much credibility and weight as you think it deserves, considering the witness's qualifications and experience, the reasons given for the opinions, and the other evidence in the case.

BURDEN OF PROOF

Burden of proof means burden of persuasion. On any claim, the party who has the burden of proof must persuade you, by the evidence, that the claim is more probably true than not true.

Breach of Contract—Elements and Damages

Plaintiff claims that Defendant Desi Dazzle breached a contract by soliciting Plaintiff's customers, by competing with it in violation of the agreement, and by disclosing its trade secrets or confidential business information. On this claim, Plaintiff must prove there was a contract with Defendant Desi Dazzle, who breached the contract, and that breach resulted in damage to Plaintiff.

To prove this claim, Plaintiff must show Defendant Desi Dazzle failed to perform an obligation under the contract that was so important to the contract that the breach defeats the purpose of the contract.

A contract is an agreement between two or more persons or entities. For a contract to exist, there must be an offer, acceptance of the offer, consideration, and terms sufficiently specific so that the obligation created by the contract can be determined. To find that the parties had a contract, you must find that they each intended to be bound by the agreement, and that they made that intention known to the other party.

[**For trials that include damages:** If you find that Defendant Desi Dazzle is liable to Plaintiff for breach of contract, you must then decide the full amount of money that will reasonably and fairly compensate Plaintiff for the damages proved by the evidence to have resulted naturally and directly from the breach of contract. The damages you award for breach of contract must be the amount of money that will place Plaintiff in the position it would have been in if the contract had been performed. To determine those damages, consider the profit Plaintiff would have received if Defendant Desi Dazzle did not breach the contract.]

Interference with Contract or Business Expectancy—Elements and Damages

Plaintiff claims that Defendants improperly interfered with its contract or business expectancy with Mega Builders, Inc. To establish this claim, Plaintiff must prove:

1. Plaintiff had a contract or business expectancy with Mega Builders, Inc.;
2. Defendants knew about the contract or business expectancy;
3. Defendants intentionally interfered with Plaintiff's contract or business expectancy with Mega Builders, Inc. resulting in a breach or termination of that contract or expectancy;

4. Defendant's conduct was improper; and

5. Plaintiff suffered damage caused by the termination of the contract or business expectancy to be realized with Mega Builders, Inc.

[**For trials that include damages:** If you find that one or more Defendants improperly interfered with Plaintiff's contract or business expectancy with Mega Builders, Inc., you must then decide the full amount of money that will reasonably and fairly compensate Plaintiff for each of the following elements of damages proved by the evidence to have resulted from the interference with the contract or business expectancy:

1. The net profit that Plaintiffs would have received had the contract been performed or the business expectancy realized; and

2. Any damage to Plaintiff's reputation.

CALCULATING LOST PROFITS

If future lost profits are reasonably certain, any reasonable basis for determining the amount of the probable profits lost is acceptable. However, the amount of lost profits cannot be based on conjecture or speculation.

In determining whether and to what extent Plaintiff proved lost profits, you must subtract the costs and expenses Plaintiff would have incurred from the gross revenue Plaintiff would have received if the contract had not been breached.]

FINAL INSTRUCTION

The case is now submitted to you for decision. When you retire to the jury room, your first task is to choose a foreperson who will preside over your deliberations.

At least seven of you must agree on a verdict. If all nine agree on a verdict, only the foreperson need sign it, on the line marked "Foreperson." If seven or eight of you agree on a verdict, all those who agree, and only those who agree, must sign the verdict on the numbered lines provided, leaving the line marked "Foreperson" blank.

SUPERIOR COURT OF NITA
DARROW COUNTY

PAT'S POOL DESIGNS, LLC Plaintiff, v. DESI DAZZLE, et al. Defendants	Case No.: CV01-67318 VERDICT FORM (liability only)

We, the jury, duly empaneled and sworn in the above-entitled cause, do find as follows:

A. Breach of Contract Claim Against Defendant Desi Dazzle

On the claim of Breach of Contract brought by Plaintiff Pat's Pool Designs, LLC against Defendant Desi Dazzle, we find:

☐ For the Plaintiff, Pat's Pool Designs, LLC

☐ For the Defendant, Desi Dazzle

B. Interference with Business Expectancy Claim Against Defendants Desi Dazzle and Delgado Pool Architects, LLC

On the claim of Interference with Business Expectancy brought by Plaintiff Pat's Pool Designs, LLC against Defendants Desi Dazzle and Delgado Pool Architects, LLC, we find:

☐ For the Plaintiff, Pat's Pool Designs, LLC

☐ For both Defendants, Desi Dazzle and Delgado Pool Architects, LLC

Dated: ______________________

Foreperson's Signature: ______________________________

SUPERIOR COURT OF NITA
DARROW COUNTY

PAT'S POOL DESIGNS, LLC Plaintiff,	Case No.: CV01-67318
v.	VERDICT FORM (use only if you find liability and are asked to determine damages)
DESI DAZZLE, et al. Defendants	

We, the jury, duly empaneled and sworn in the above-entitled cause, assess the following damages:

If you found in favor of the Plaintiff on the **Breach of Contract** claim:

Damages awarded to Plaintiff on this claim: $________________

If you found in favor of the Plaintiff on the **Interference with Business Expectancy** claim:

Damages awarded to Plaintiff on this claim: $________________

* If you find for Plaintiff on both claims, you may award damages separately for each claim, but the total damages must not duplicate any amounts.

Dated: ______________________

Foreperson's Signature: ______________________________

Optional Motion Materials

Plaintiff's Attorney
123 Central Avenue
Nita City, Nita 85013

SUPERIOR COURT OF NITA
DARROW COUNTY

PAT'S POOL DESIGNS, LLC Plaintiff, v. DESI DAZZLE, et al. Defendants	Case No.: CV01-67318 PLAINTIFF'S APPLICATION FOR PRELIMINARY INJUNCTION

Pat's Pool Designs, LLC seeks narrowly tailored injunctive relief to stop an ongoing raid on its customer and employee relationships and the continued misuse of its confidential business information by former executive Desi Dazzle and Dazzle's new employer, Delgado Pool Architects, LLC ("Delgado"). The relief sought is exactly what Plaintiff and Dazzle agreed to—it is limited, time-bound, and designed to preserve the status quo pending trial.

FACTUAL BACKGROUND

Pat's Pool Designs ("Pat's") has long been a fixture in Nita City's high-end pool design market. Led by owner and president Lynn Lasery, the company built a reputation for delivering custom projects and maintaining enduring client relationships. In September of YR-10, Pat's hired Desi Dazzle as a salesperson, later promoting Dazzle to vice president of sales in YR-5. As part of onboarding and promotion, Dazzle signed, and initialed, several restrictive covenants: a nonsolicitation of employees and customers, a noncompete, and a confidentiality provision protecting Pat's nonpublic information (Complaint ¶¶17–23; Ex. 1). Dazzle does not dispute agreeing to these terms (Dazzle Depo).

Pat's considered its customer information to be highly sensitive: not just names and addresses, but relationship-specific details such as preferences, birthdays, and family information, as well as pricing histories and project concepts. Lasery and the Pat's sales team cultivated this data over years, and it became a central asset for winning repeat business (Complaint ¶¶19, 21; Lasery Depo).

In the fall of YR-2, Pat's was deep into negotiations for a major project: the Mega Builders, Inc. development, involving 210 residential pools and 3 community pools. On October 31, YR-2, Mega Builders and Pat's signed a letter of intent, reflecting a $13.15 million price and early-payment incentives, and committing to work in good faith toward a final contract (Ex. 2, LOI). Although the LOI was nonbinding, Pat's believed the deal was essentially secured (Snyder Depo). Dazzle signed the LOI on Pat's behalf due to the absence of CFO Allen Snyder.

That same day and in the days immediately following, Dazzle began corresponding with Domi Gianni, owner of Delgado Pool Architects. Emails from October 31 to November 2 show Dazzle expressing frustration with the VP of sales role at Pat's and a desire to discuss opportunities at Delgado (Ex. 3). Within weeks, Dazzle decided to make the move, resigning from Pat's on December 7, YR-2 (Ex. 3, Email 4; Dazzle Depo). Dazzle began as Delgado vice president of sales on January 3 (Dazzle Depo; Gianni Depo).

Lasery promptly notified Gianni, on January 5 and 6, of Dazzle's restrictive covenants, attaching Pat's employee handbook, highlighting the pertinent covenants, and warning about the nonsolicitation, noncompete, and confidentiality obligations (Ex. 4). By then, however, Dazzle had already suggested to Gianni that Delgado pursue the Mega Builders opportunity. Acting on that suggestion, Delgado submitted its own proposal using a pricing model Dazzle developed at Pat's. According to Gianni, Mega Builders instructed Delgado to draw up a contract before year-end, and the deal was signed on December 30, YR-2 (Gianni Depo).

The fallout of Dazzle's betrayal was swift for Pat's. In January YR-1, Mega Builders informed Pat's that it had chosen another company (Ex. 6; Snyder Depo). Soon after, two of Pat's architects, MJ Barr and Monique Carter, resigned. In exit interviews, both indicated Dazzle had contacted them about positions at Delgado, offering what they described as "too good to pass up" (Lasery Depo). At around the same time, long-standing pool maintenance and servicing clients including Haden Hotels and Rocker Resorts shifted their business to Delgado. Dazzle acknowledges sending messages to those clients after starting at Delgado, highlighting this new position and Delgado's capabilities (Dazzle Depo).

These events—Dazzle's immediate solicitation of Pat's employees and customers, involvement in diverting Mega Builders, and use of relationship-specific information gained at Pat's—all caused serious harm to Pat's goodwill and competitive standing. The loss of the Mega Builders project, coupled with key staff departures and client erosion, created ripple effects in lost referrals, diminished employee morale, and damaged Pat's market position (Lasery Depo).

A preliminary injunction is an extraordinary remedy granted upon a clear showing that the movant is entitled to such relief. *Winter v. Nat. Res. Def. Council, Inc.*, 555 U.S. 7, 20 (2008). *Winter* held that, to obtain a preliminary injunction, the movant must establish:

(1) a likelihood of success on the merits;

(2) a likelihood of suffering irreparable harm absent the injunction;

(3) that the balance of equities tips in the movant's favor; and

(4) that an injunction is in the public interest.

LIKELIHOOD OF SUCCESS ON THE MERITS

Pat's is likely to prevail on its contract claims because each restrictive covenant is reasonable in time, geography, and scope, and each was breached.

A. Nonsolicitation of Employees (twelve months)—Enforceable and Breached

The first nonsolicitation clause bars Dazzle for twelve months post-employment from directly or indirectly soliciting Pat's employees or assisting others to do so (Ex. 1, §2.1, Nonsolicitation [employees/vendors]). The covenant targets workforce stability, a classic, legitimate interest, and is narrowly time-limited to one year.

Within weeks of Dazzle's resignation and start at Delgado, two key Pat's architects, MJ Barr and Monique Carter, departed for Delgado. Lasery reports both said Dazzle had reached out both of them about opportunities that were "too good to pass" (Lasery Depo). Dazzle confirms sharing compensation and work-environment details and passing their information to Gianni (Dazzle Depo). This is actionable solicitation under the covenant.

The covenant does not bar ordinary employment elsewhere; it narrowly proscribes active recruitment of Pat's staff for a brief period. Given the relationship-centric nature of Pat's business and the timing of the departures, the clause is reasonably tailored to protect Pat's investment in its team, and injunctive enforcement simply restores the pre-breach status quo.

B. Nonsolicitation of Customers (six months; limited class)—Enforceable and Breached

The second nonsolicitation provision bars Dazzle for six months from soliciting or providing design/installation services to (i) any person or entity that was a Pat's customer at the time of termination and (ii) who does business within five miles of Nita City's town limits (Ex. 1, §2.1, Non-Solicitation [customers]). It is limited to customers Dazzle just worked with and to Pat's core local market.

Dazzle admits post-departure contact with Haden Hotels and Rocker Resorts touting Delgado's reliability and Dazzle's new role; those accounts later shifted to Delgado (Dazzle Depo; Gianni Depo). The timing and content of the outreach support a customer-solicitation breach. As to Mega Builders, while the LOI was nonbinding, Dazzle's coordination with Delgado to submit a competing proposal immediately after resignation, leveraging insight from Pat's pursuit, further evidences solicitation aimed at a then-active Pat's prospective customer.

The provision is tightly drawn—six months, existing customers only, and a small, five-mile footprint. It does not bar Dazzle from working in the industry, only from targeting Pat's active accounts in Pat's immediate market during a short cooling-off period.

C. Noncompete (six months; five-mile radius; existing customers only)—Enforceable and Breached

The noncompete bars Dazzle for six months from soliciting or providing pool design/installation services to any Pat's customer who does business within five miles of Nita City (Ex. 1, §2.1, Noncompetition). It is expressly customer-bound and geography-limited; it does not prohibit Dazzle from working for Delgado, pursuing new customers outside the five-mile area, or serving non-Pat's customers.

Immediately after resigning, Dazzle joined Delgado as VP of sales and engaged with Pat's customer and prospective-customer base in the same local market—including outreach connected to Mega Builders and communications with Haden Hotels and Rocker Resorts. This conduct falls within the noncompete's customer-bound, five-mile limitation.

A six-month, five-mile, existing-customer-only restraint is a modest temporal and geographic protection calibrated to Pat's local book of business and the relationship-transfer risk an executive sales leader poses at departure.

D. Confidentiality—Enforceable and Breached

The confidentiality covenant prohibits using or disclosing Pat's nonpublic business information, including customer lists, preference data, and business methods (Ex. 1, §2.1, Nondisclosure).

Dazzle acknowledges maintaining personal contact information and "extra information" (birthdays, kids' names, coffee orders, hobbies) about Pat's customers and coworkers on a private cellphone/calendar and continuing to communicate with them after resigning (Dazzle Depo). Dazzle also advised Delgado to pursue Mega Builders using pricing concepts Dazzle had advocated at Pat's (Dazzle & Gianni Depos). Using Pat's relationship intelligence and know-how to target Pat's accounts violates the confidentiality covenant even absent physical file-taking.

IRREPARABLE HARM

The record shows ongoing loss of goodwill and destabilized relationships with employees and customers, including a flagship program (Mega Builders) and smaller but reputationally important pool maintenance and servicing accounts (Haden Hotels, Rocker Resorts). Those losses produce cascading effects impacting future renewals, referrals, and upgrade revenue that cannot be reliably calculated at this stage. Absent an injunction, continued use of Pat's relationship intelligence and solicitation will compound the harm.

Loss of goodwill, customer relationships, and key employees constitutes irreparable harm. These harms are difficult to quantify, ongoing, and not compensable solely by money damages. Continued use of Pat's trade secrets by Defendants threatens permanent erosion of Plaintiff's competitive advantage.

BALANCE OF EQUITIES AND PUBLIC INTEREST

The harm to Pat's from continued violations far outweighs any hardship to Defendants from being ordered to comply with their legal obligations. Defendants have no legitimate interest in soliciting Pat's customers and employees using Pat's confidential information.

The public interest is served by enforcing valid contracts, protecting trade secrets, and discouraging unfair competition.

RELIEF REQUESTED

Plaintiff respectfully requests that this Court enter a Preliminary Injunction:

1. Enjoin Defendants for twelve months from directly or indirectly soliciting, recruiting, hiring, or inducing any current Pat's employee;

2. Enjoin Defendants for six months from soliciting or providing design/installation services to any Pat's customer that (a) was a Pat's customer at Dazzle's departure and (b) does business within five miles of Nita City;

3. Enjoin Defendants from using or disclosing Pat's confidential/nonpublic information; require immediate return and deletion of such information with certifications;

4. Permit responses to unsolicited inquiries and participation in public RFPs, provided no use of Pat's confidential information; and

5. Set the injunction to expire per the contractual durations and require a nominal bond given the tailored relief.

Dated this ____________________

____

[ATTORNEY NAME]

Defendants' Attorney
123 Main Street
Nita City, Nita 85032

SUPERIOR COURT OF NITA
DARROW COUNTY

PAT'S POOL DESIGNS, LLC Plaintiff, v. DESI DAZZLE, et al. Defendants	Case No.: CV01-67318 DEFENDANT'S OPPOSITION TO THE PLAINTIFF'S APPLICATION FOR PRELIMINARY INJUNCTION

Plaintiff asks the Court to impose extraordinary restraints that would sideline a competitor and prevent a former employee from using their skills in the open market. The record does not justify that relief. The Mega Builders letter of intent was expressly nonbinding (Ex. 2, LOI), Plaintiff's restrictive covenants sweep far beyond any legitimate interest (Ex. 1), and the claimed harms are ordinary, measurable business losses tied to a competitive award, a few staff moves, and some client churn. Because Plaintiff cannot show a likelihood of success on the merits, irreparable harm, or that the equities and public interest favor an injunction, the application should be denied.

A preliminary injunction is an "extraordinary remedy" that may be granted only upon a "clear showing" that the movant satisfies all four elements:

(1) likelihood of success on the merits,

(2) likelihood of irreparable harm absent relief,

(3) the balance of equities in the movant's favor, and

(4) service of the public interest.

Winter v. Nat. Res. Def. Council, Inc., 555 U.S. 7, 20 (2008).

BACKGROUND

Pat's Pool Designs ("Pat's") is a pool design and installation firm owned by Lynn Lasery (Complaint ¶¶9–16). Pat's hired Desi Dazzle as a salesperson on September 11, YR-10 and later promoted Dazzle to vice president of sales in YR-5. As a condition of employment, Dazzle signed standard-form restrictive covenants addressing noncompetition, non-solicitation of employees and customers, and confidentiality (Complaint ¶¶17–23; Ex. 1). Dazzle initialed the key provisions and does not dispute the signature on the document (Dazzle Depo).

In the fall of YR-2, Pat's was pursuing a large opportunity: Mega Builders' development of 210 residential pools plus 3 community installations. On October 31, YR-2, Pat's and Mega Builders executed a letter of intent ("LOI") setting forth target pricing and an agreement to negotiate in good faith toward a formal contract. The LOI states that it is nonbinding and anticipates that any definitive agreement would be set out in a later contract (Ex. 2, LOI). Allen Snyder, Pat's CFO, led the bid effort; Dazzle signed the LOI for Pat's when Snyder was unavailable (Snyder Depo; Ex. 2).

That same week, Dazzle exchanged emails with Domi Gianni, the owner of Delgado Pool Architects ("Delgado"), expressing frustration about Dazzle's position at Pat's and openness to a discussion about joining Delgado (Ex. 3, Emails Oct. 31–Nov. 2). Dazzle resigned from Pat's on December 7, YR-2 (Ex. 3, Email 4; Dazzle Depo) and began at Delgado as vice president of sales on January 3, YR-1 (Dazzle Depo; Gianni Depo). On January 5, Lasery emailed Gianni copies of the relevant handbook excerpts and highlighted Dazzle's post-employment restrictions (Ex. 4).

In the window between the LOI and year end, Mega Builders invited a competing proposal. Delgado submitted its own bid—Gianni testifies that it used Delgado's pricing and terms—and states Mega Builders instructed Delgado to finalize a contract before year-end. According to Gianni, the contract with Mega Builders was signed on December 30, YR-2 (Gianni Depo). In early January YR-1, Mega Builders notified Pat's that another company had been chosen (Texts, Exs. 5–6; Snyder Depo).

Around the same period, two of Pat's architects, MJ Barr and Monique Carter, left Pat's and later joined Delgado. Pat's exit interviews attribute the departures to Dazzle's outreach (Lasery Depo), while Dazzle and Gianni state that Barr and Carter approached or applied to Delgado based on publicly posted openings and better compensation (Dazzle Depo; Gianni Depo). Some smaller accounts—including Haden Hotels and Rocker Resorts—shifted their pool maintenance and servicing to Delgado. Dazzle acknowledges sending messages after starting at Delgado. These messages announced Dazzle's new role and Delgado's capabilities (Dazzle Depo).

Plaintiff characterizes its customer information as confidential "relationship intelligence," including birthdays, family details, and preferences. Plaintiff identifies no specific file or database that Dazzle took or retained; Dazzle denies taking documents. Instead, Dazzle avers relying on general industry knowledge and personally gleaned information about these contacts (Dazzle Depo). Gianni states Delgado's bid to Mega Builders reflected Delgado's own pricing and approach and was not based on Pat's documents (Gianni Depo).

LIKELIHOOD OF SUCCESS

A. The Restrictive Covenant Is Overly Broad and Unenforceable

All of the restrictive covenants Plaintiff seeks to enforce suffer from the same fatal flaws: they are drafted so broadly that they function as restraints on ordinary competition, and Plaintiff has not produced evidence showing that Dazzle's post-employment conduct falls within any legitimate, protectable scope.

The employee nonsolicitation clause sweeps in "any" Pat's employee for a full twelve months, with no limitation to employees in whom Pat's has invested specialized training, who possess confidential information, or who worked under Dazzle's supervision (Ex. 1, §2.1). Such an undifferentiated ban operates as a blanket labor market restraint. The only evidence of solicitation comes from exit interview summaries by Lasery; Dazzle and Gianni attest that the two architects who left, MJ Barr and Monique Carter, applied for publicly posted positions at Delgado for higher compensation and better career prospects (Dazzle Depo; Gianni Depo).

The customer nonsolicitation covenant is likewise overinclusive. It prohibits Dazzle for six months from soliciting or providing services to "any" Pat's customer as of termination if the customer "does business within five miles of Nita City" (Ex. 1, §2.1). This restriction is not tied to customers with whom Dazzle had direct contact or built goodwill, and the geographic trigger is vague for multi-location clients. Plaintiff's proof consists of Dazzle's general announcement messages on social media that were seen by Haden Hotels and Rocker Resorts, which Dazzle says led to competitive bidding or unsolicited inquiries (Dazzle Depo). As to Mega Builders, the October 31 LOI was expressly nonbinding (Ex. 2) and did not bar any competitor from bidding. The noncompete provision, which bars Dazzle for six months from serving any Pat's customer doing business within five miles of Nita City, is effectively a market-wide restraint as applied. It is not limited to customers tied to Dazzle's goodwill or to projects at genuine risk of diversion. Plaintiff seeks to apply it to Mega Builders and other accounts based merely on their incidental business within the radius. The record shows Delgado won Mega Builders through its own proposal after an open, competitive process (Giannrini Depo; Ex. 2).

Finally, the confidentiality clause, while narrower in concept, has not been shown to be breached. Plaintiff has not identified any specific document or file that Dazzle took or used after leaving. Dazzle denies retaining any materials, and both Dazzle and Gianni state Delgado's Mega Builders proposal reflected Delgado's own pricing and terms. Plaintiff's allegation that these bids relied on database information such as birthdays and spouses' names neither equates misuse of confidential business records nor reflects the reality of the "relationship intelligence" personally recorded by Dazzle.

Taken together, these covenants reach far beyond any legitimate interest in protecting customer goodwill, confidential information, or workforce stability. Applied as Plaintiff urges, they would prevent Dazzle from engaging in lawful competition for a broad, ill-defined class of employees and customers. On this record, they are not enforceable.

B. There Was No Contract to Interfere With

The letter of intent between Pat's Pools and Mega Builders, signed on October 31, YR-2, was expressly nonbinding and subject to execution of a formal contract "in the coming weeks" (LOI). No such contract was executed. Without a binding agreement, Plaintiff cannot sustain a claim for tortious interference.

ANY DAMAGE IS EASILY REDRESSED IN MONEY DAMAGES

Plaintiff's claimed injuries are quintessentially economic: the profit on Mega Builders (if any), the cost of replacing two architects, and margin changes from clients that shifted work. Those can be calculated from bid worksheets, historical margins, payroll records, and account histories (Snyder Depo). Plaintiff's invocation of "goodwill" is conclusory; it offers no competent evidence tying brand erosion or future churn to Defendants' conduct as opposed to normal competitive dynamics. The timing also undercuts any emergency; key events occurred in late YR-2 and early YR-1, weeks before filing.

EQUITY AND PUBLIC POLICY FAVOR DENYING THE APPLICATION

An injunction would prevent Defendants from engaging in lawful competition, restrict Dazzle from using any general skills and experience, and penalize Delgado for pursuing opportunities that were not contractually committed to Plaintiff. Any hardship to Plaintiff is compensable in damages; the hardship to Defendants from an injunction is not.

The public interest favors employee mobility, lawful competition, and enforcement of reasonable, not overreaching, restraints. Extending and expanding an already overbroad noncompete chills legitimate market competition and undermines consumer choice.

Dated this______________________

____
[ATTORNEY NAME]

Optional Expert Materials

REPORT OF DR. JAMIE CALDWELL, PHD—ECONOMIC CONSULTANT PREPARED FOR COUNSEL REPRESENTING PAT'S POOL DESIGNS, LLC

I. Summary of Opinions

This expert report provides a comprehensive analysis of the economic damages incurred by Pat's Pool Designs, LLC ("Pat's") as a direct result of alleged trade secret misappropriation, breach of contract, and tortious interference by Desi Dazzle and Delgado Pool Architects, LLC ("Defendants"). I conclude, to a reasonable degree of economic certainty, that Pat's has suffered a total present value loss of approximately $5,135,606. This amount consists of $3,945,000 in direct lost profits from the failed Mega Builders project and $1,190,606 in future business losses discounted to present value.

The damage estimates are based on a combination of historical company financials, industry-standard economic modeling, and a causal analysis of customer attrition patterns following Desi Dazzle's departure. Each figure is grounded in reliable data and adjusted using conservative economic assumptions.

II. Economic Basis for Lost Profits

A. Mega Builders Project and Revenue Expectation

The anticipated Mega Builders project was set to generate $13.15 million in gross revenue. This figure was supported by a signed letter of intent (LOI), followed by corroborating emails, design drafts, and scheduled meetings. While the LOI is technically nonbinding, in practice, such documents frequently indicate a near-finalized agreement in the commercial construction industry, particularly when significant steps have already been undertaken.

It is common in custom pool architecture and engineering contracts for LOIs to evolve into full contracts once final design and permitting stages are completed. In this case, the sequence of business actions and communications would reasonably lead to final execution absent the alleged interference.

B. Profit Margin Assumptions

Pat's Pool Designs historically earned an average gross profit margin of 30 percent across its commercial contracts, supported by five years of financial statements and CPA-reviewed filings. This margin is within range for specialized design-build service firms, especially those offering proprietary engineering services.

Multiplying the $13.15 million project revenue by the 30 percent margin results in $3,945,000 in lost profits attributable directly to the thwarted Mega Builders engagement.

III. Future Losses from Client Attrition and Market Harm

1. Post-Departure Revenue Decline

Following Desi Dazzle's resignation and subsequent affiliation with Delgado Pool Architects, Pat's experienced a significant reduction in inquiries and new contract conversions. Based on CRM data and client exit interviews, it was determined that several longstanding clients pivoted to Delgado, citing both product innovation and engineering quality they previously associated with Pat's.

This customer migration supports a conclusion that proprietary designs or methods may have been utilized by the Defendants, compounding the damages through market share erosion.

2. Future Revenue Forecasting

Using conservative forecasting based on trailing twelve-month sales data, adjusted for historical customer retention trends, I project an annual loss of approximately $275,000 in foregone earnings over a five-year period. This cumulative figure of $1,375,000 was subjected to risk adjustment and a 5 percent annual discount rate, yielding a present value of $1,190,606.

The 5 percent discount rate is aligned with mid-tier risk commercial business projections, consistent with market practice when estimating lost future income. This assumption reflects the relative stability of Pat's prior earnings and its established customer base.

IV. Response to Defense Expert (Dr. Stephen Marks)

1. Letter of Intent Validity

Dr. Marks asserts the LOI has no legal weight. While accurate legally, this view fails to recognize that in commercial practice, an LOI often represents a strong indicator of mutual commitment. Courts evaluating economic damages often consider the economic reality of such instruments, especially when supported by evidence of ongoing reliance and preparation.

2. Profit Margin Discrepancy

Dr. Marks reduces expected profits by applying a 20 percent margin. However, he provides no firm basis for this substitution. Pat's verified 30 percent average profit on past jobs of similar scope is more reliable than speculative industry averages. Dr. Marks's margin reduction lacks empirical grounding specific to this firm's operating model.

3. Minimizing Future Losses

Dr. Marks discounts future client attrition by suggesting multiple potential causes. However, my findings are not speculative. They are supported by customer exit data and temporal correlation with the Defendants' competitive entry. Additionally, attributing all attrition to "market competition" ignores the potential misuse of proprietary design methods.

4. Discount Rate Inflation

Applying an 8 percent discount rate to future earnings reflects an overly high-risk profile not consistent with Pat's established track record. A 5 percent rate more appropriately reflects Pat's historical performance and the relative predictability of its earnings prior to the defendant's actions.

V. Conclusion

Based on empirical financial data, established economic methods, and customer impact analysis, I conclude that Pat's Pool Designs has suffered total present-value damages of $5,135,606. This includes $3,945,000 in direct lost profits from the failed Mega Builders project and $1,190,606 in discounted future earnings losses stemming from customer attrition.

These figures are well-supported, economically justifiable, and grounded in reliable projections. The analysis directly rebuts the defense's claim of speculative forecasting and instead presents a balanced, evidence-based assessment of economic harm incurred.

Dr. Jamie Caldwell, PhD

Professor of Economics

Email: jcaldwell@uchicago.edu | Phone: (819) 555-2025

Education

Ph.D., Economics, University of Chicago, YR-19

M.A., Applied Mathematics, Princeton University, YR-23

B.S., Quantitative Economics, Massachusetts Institute of Technology, YR-21

Academic Positions

Professor of Economics, University of Chicago, YR-11–Present

Associate Professor, University of Michigan, YR-17–YR-11

Assistant Professor, University of Michigan, YR-19–YR-17

Research Interests

- Economic modeling of contract disputes
- Valuation of intellectual property
- Firm behavior under uncertainty

Publications

Caldwell, J. (YR-1), 'Behavioral Economics in Contract Negotiations,' *Journal of Law & Economics*

Caldwell, J. (YR-2), 'Discounting Future Profits in Trade Secret Litigation,' *Journal of Legal Economics*

Caldwell, J. (YR-4), 'Estimating Lost Profits with Imperfect Information,' *Review of Economic Studies*

Caldwell, J. (YR-6), 'The Economic Role of Noncompete Agreements,' *American Economic Review*

Conference Presentations & Invited Talks

- Keynote Speaker, 'Economic Damages in IP Litigation,' International Economic Law Symposium, YR-2
- Presenter, 'Modeling Lost Profits in Emerging Industries,' AEA Annual Meeting, YR-3
- Panel Chair, 'Quantitative Methods in Law & Economics,' University of Chicago, YR-4

Expert Witness Experience

Testifying expert in multiple cases involving contract valuation, IP disputes, and market analysis. Reports and testimony accepted in both U.S. District Courts and arbitration panels.

REPORT OF DR. STEPHEN MARKS, CPA—FINANCIAL ANALYST PREPARED FOR COUNSEL REPRESENTING DELGADO POOL ARCHITECTS, LLC

I. Summary of Findings

This report provides a structured rebuttal to the economic damages claim submitted by Dr. Jamie Caldwell on behalf of Pat's Pool Designs, LLC ("Pat's"). Based on a thorough review of market data, contract law implications, and accepted financial methodologies, I conclude that the alleged economic damages claimed by Pat's are materially overstated, rely on speculative forecasting, and do not reflect appropriate levels of risk or contract uncertainty.

The estimated damages of $5,135,606 presented by Dr. Caldwell are not supported by binding contractual obligations or demonstrated loss causation. After correcting for profit margin overstatements, adjusting for actual market behavior, and applying a risk-aligned discount rate, I estimate that maximum plausible economic damages should not exceed $3,571,725, and may in fact be substantially lower.

II. Evaluation of the Mega Builders Engagement

1. Nonbinding Nature of the Agreement

The letter of intent (LOI) between Pat's and Mega Builders, while indicative of preliminary interest, explicitly stated that it was nonbinding and subject to further agreement. In commercial practice, such LOIs are considered aspirational, particularly in industries such as construction where detailed specifications, permits, and contractual milestones are prerequisites to contract finalization.

There is no executed agreement, no invoice or payment schedule, and no record of commitment to commence work. As such, claims based on the assumption that this contract was "certain" lack the necessary legal and economic foundation to support damages.

2. Profitability Assumptions

Dr. Caldwell relies on a 30 percent gross profit margin, allegedly based on Pat's historical performance. However, industry benchmarks for comparable design-and-build commercial pool projects suggest average gross margins in the range of 18 percent to 22 percent. In light of increased input costs, labor variability, and market competition, assuming a 30 percent margin is overly optimistic.

Applying a more conservative 20 percent margin to the $13.15 million earnings figure produces a revised direct lost profit estimate of $2,630,000, which I consider a generous upper bound given the speculative nature of the underlying contract.

III. Evaluation of Future Loss Claims

1. Causation and Alternative Explanations

Dr. Caldwell attributes future losses primarily to customer attrition following Desi Dazzle's departure. However, CRM data, as cited, may not reflect a full causal picture. Pat's had existing operational inefficiencies, employee dissatisfaction, which could have independently contributed to declining client retention.

Furthermore, some client loss may reflect market shifts and evolving customer preferences. Attribution of loss solely to the defendant's actions is, therefore, economically unjustified.

2. Quantifying Future Losses

Dr. Caldwell's forecast of $1.375 million in future lost earnings over five years assumes stable pricing, zero recovery in client base, and a linear loss pattern. These assumptions disregard normal business recovery cycles, competitive repositioning, and adaptation.

I have applied a 25 percent recovery assumption (assuming 5 percent of customers are recovered each year over the five-year period) to the projected loss stream, which reduces expected losses to approximately $1,168,750. I then apply an 8 percent discount rate, which reflects the higher uncertainty inherent in small business projections involving brand damage, market competition, and intangible asset valuation. This yields a present value of approximately $941,725.

IV. Economic and Risk Considerations

1. Appropriate Discounting Methodology

Discount rates should reflect the riskiness of projected cash flows. Dr. Caldwell's use of a 5 percent rate underestimates the volatility and business risk associated with Pat's operations, especially post-allegation. The firm's modest size, narrow client base, and reliance on key personnel increase the cost of capital and risk profile.

A more appropriate rate is 8 percent to 10 percent, in line with SBA estimates and private capital markets for comparable firms.

2. Speculative Nature of Competitive Harm

Dr. Caldwell relies on customer testimony and temporal coincidence to allege misappropriation. However, no forensic analysis of proprietary information is presented. In absence of such proof, market loss could equally result from innovation by Delgado Pool Architects or better customer targeting, both lawful competitive practices.

V. Rebuttal Summary

Letter of Intent: Legally and economically nonbinding; no foundation for certain damages.

Profit Margin: Industry norms suggest 20 percent gross margin, not 30 percent.

Customer Loss: Attributable to multiple factors; causality not proven.

Discount Rate: A higher rate (8 percent) is appropriate given risk profile.

Future Losses: Speculative and assume unrealistic static conditions.

VI. Conclusion

My economic analysis, grounded in conservative valuation practices and legal-commercial realities, finds that Pat's Pool Designs' claimed damages are significantly inflated. A legally uncertain contract, market-based client shifts, and unproven misuse of proprietary information undermine the magnitude of loss asserted.

The more defensible estimate of total economic damages is $3,571,725 or less, composed of $2,630,000 in possible lost profits and $941,725 in present value of future losses. These findings reflect reasonable, market-aligned methodologies and are based on empirical financial modeling rather than hypothetical projections.

Respectfully submitted,

Dr. Stephen Marks, CPA

Stephen Marks, CPA, CVA

Email: stephen@marksecon.nita | Phone: (819) 555-3344 |
Linque: linque.nita/in/stephenmarks

Professional Summary

Experienced Certified Public Accountant and Certified Valuation Analyst with over 25 years in forensic accounting, economic damages analysis, and valuation services. Known for providing clear, defensible opinions in high-stakes commercial litigation and arbitration.

Education & Certifications

B.S. in Accounting, Indiana University, YR-30
Certified Public Accountant (CPA)
Certified Valuation Analyst (CVA)
Annual CPE in Litigation Support, Valuation, and Forensic Accounting

Professional Experience

Managing Partner, Marks Economic Advisors (YR-15–Present)

Lead economic damages consultant for complex business disputes; authored over 100 detailed expert reports and provided testimony in more than 60 trials and arbitrations.

Director of Litigation Support, Midwest Financial Consulting (YR-25–YR-15)

Managed forensic accounting investigations, calculated lost profits, and developed rebuttal reports for *Fortune* 500 and mid-market companies.

Audit Manager, BDO Seidman LLP (YR-30–YR-25)

Directed audit teams for publicly traded and private companies across manufacturing, construction, and service industries.

Selected Expert Engagements

- Testified in $150M IP valuation dispute in U.S. District Court (YR-2)
- Rebuttal expert in $80M construction delay claim involving multi-state contractors (YR-3)
- Lead valuation expert for merger dispute between technology firms (YR-4)

Publications

- "Assessing Economic Damages in Emerging Tech Markets," *Litigation Economics Journal*, YR-3
- "Forensic Accounting in Post-Merger Disputes," *Journal of Business Valuation*, YR-5

Speaking Engagements

- Panelist, "Valuation Trends in IP Litigation," ABA Section of Litigation Annual Conference, YR-2
- Speaker, "Economic Damages in the Construction Sector," AICPA Forensic & Valuation Services Conference, YR-3

Special Impeachment Problems

Special Impeachment Problems for Plaintiff

Assume the witnesses testify as follows. Impeach the witnesses based on their statements.

1. Domi Gianni testifies at trial: "I had never heard of Desi Dazzle before the builders conference in YR-2."

   Impeachment source: Gianni Deposition, p. 17, lines 14–17

2. Domi Gianni testifies at trial: "Desi never mentioned the Mega Builders project to me before joining Delgado."

   Impeachment source: Gianni Deposition, p. 17, lines 41–42

3. Domi Gianni testifies at trial: "Delgado only started negotiating with Mega Builders after Desi officially began working for us."

   Impeachment source: Gianni Deposition, p. 17, lines 38–39 and page 18, lines 4–5

4. Domi Gianni testifies at trial: "None of Pat's employees ever contacted us about working at Delgado."

   Impeachment source: Gianni Deposition, p. 18, lines 10–15

5. Lynn Lasery testifies at trial: "I prepared all of the policies and employment agreements we used at Pat's Pools myself."

   Impeachment source: Lasery Deposition, p. 19, lines 7–9

6. Lynn Lasery testifies at trial: "I always intended Desi to lead the Mega Builders negotiations."

   Impeachment source: Lasery Deposition, p. 20, lines 17–19

7. Lynn Lasery testifies at trial: "When Desi resigned, they explicitly promised me they would abide by the restrictive covenants in the contract."

   Impeachment source: Lasery Deposition, p. 20, lines 38–41

8. Lynn Lasery testifies at trial: "Our contacts at Haden Hotels and Rocker's Resorts said Desi reached out to them to lure them away from us and to Delgado."

   Impeachment source: Lasery Deposition, p. 21, lines 8–11

Special Impeachment Problems for Defendant

Assume the witnesses testify as follows. Impeach the witnesses based on their statements.

1. Desi Dazzle testifies at trial: "I don't recognize the initials on Exhibit 1, the noncompete and confidentiality provisions of my contract with Pat's Pool Designs."

   Impeachment source: Dazzle Deposition, p. 11, lines 10–12

2. Desi Dazzle testifies at trial: "I led the negotiations with Mega Builders and developed the proposal that Pat's presented."

   Impeachment source: Dazzle Deposition, p. 11, lines 27–30

3. Desi Dazzle testifies at trial: "My method of upselling made Pat's over $35 million in the years I was there."

   Impeachment source: Dazzle Deposition, p. 12, lines 8–9

4. Desi Dazzle testifies at trial: "I never talked to anyone at Delgado about my ideas for pricing and product enhancements until I started working there on January 3, YR-1."

   Impeachment source: Dazzle Deposition, p. 13, lines 7–8

5. Allen Snyder testifies at trial: "I was only minimally involved in preparing the Mega Builders proposal."

   Impeachment source: Snyder Deposition, p. 15, lines 10–13

6. Allen Snyder testifies at trial: "I had no personal stake in the outcome of the negotiations with Mega Builders."

   Impeachment source: Snyder Deposition, p. 15, lines 21–22 or page 16: lines 10–11

7. Allen Snyder testifies at trial: "I was present when the letter of intent with Mega Builders was signed."

   Impeachment source: Snyder Deposition, p. 15, lines 39–40

8. Allen Snyder testifies at trial: "I felt sorry for Desi but never got upset with Desi. I always said, 'we both share all the credit for landing Mega Builders.'"

   Impeachment source: Snyder Deposition, p. 16, lines 3–4

www.ingramcontent.com/pod-product-compliance
Lightning Source LLC
LaVergne TN
LVHW082358200926
848481LV00012B/3599